Nittany Lionology Trivia Challenge

Penn State Nittany Lions Football

**Nittany Lionology Trivia Challenge – Penn State Nittany Lions Football;
First Edition 2008**

Published by
Kick The Ball, Ltd
8595 Columbus Pike, Suite 197
Lewis Center, OH 43035
www.TriviaGameBooks.com

Designed, Formatted, and Edited by: Tom P. Rippey III & Paul F. Wilson
Researched by: Tom P. Rippey III

*For information on ordering this book in bulk at reduced prices, please email us
at pfwilson@trivianthology.com.*

International Standard Book Number: 978-1-934372-41-8

Printed & Bound in the United States of America

Tom P. Rippey III & Paul F. Wilson

Nittany Lionology Trivia Challenge

Penn State Nittany Lions Football

Researched by Tom P. Rippey III

Tom P. Rippey III & Paul F. Wilson, Editors

Kick The Ball, Ltd
Lewis Center, Ohio

This book is dedicated to our families and friends for your unwavering love, support, and your understanding of our pursuit of our passions. Thank you for everything you do for us and for making our lives complete.

Dear Friend,

Thank you for purchasing our **Nittany Lionology Trivia Challenge** game book!

We hope you enjoy it as much as we enjoyed researching and putting it together. This book can be used over and over again in many different ways. One example would be to use it in a head-to-head challenge by alternating questions between Nittany Lion football fans – or by playing as teams. Another option would be to simply challenge yourself to see how many questions you could answer correctly. No matter how you choose to use this book, you'll have fun and maybe even learn a fact or two about Nittany Lions football.

We have made every attempt to verify the accuracy of the questions and answers contained in this book. However it is still possible that from time to time an error has been made by us or our researchers. In the event you find a question or answer that is questionable or inaccurate, we ask for your understanding and thank you for bringing it to our attention so that we may improve future editions of this book. Please email us at tprippey@trivianthology.com with those observations and comments.

Have fun playing **Nittany Lionology Trivia Challenge**!

Tom & Paul

Tom Rippey & Paul Wilson
Co-Founders, Kick The Ball, Ltd

PS – You can discover more about all of our current trivia game books by visiting us online at www.TriviaGameBooks.com.

Table of Contents

NITTANY LIONOLOGY TRIVIA CHALLENGE

How to Play

Book Format:

There are four quarters, each made up of fifty questions. Each quarter's questions have assigned point values. Questions are designed to get progressively more difficult as you proceed through each quarter, as well as through the book itself. Most questions are in a four-option multiple-choice format so that you will at least have a 25% chance of getting a correct answer for some of the more challenging questions.

We've even added an *Overtime* section in the event of a tie, or just in case you want to keep playing a little longer.

Game Options:

One Player -
To play on your own, simply answer each of the questions in all the quarters, and in the overtime section, if you'd like. Use the *Player / Team Score Sheet* to record your answers and the quarter *Answer Keys* to check your answers. Calculate each quarter's points and the total for the game at the bottom of the *Player / Team Score Sheet* to determine your final score.

Two or More Players –
To play with multiple players decide if you will all be competing with each other individually, or if you will form and play as teams. Each player / team will then have its own *Player / Team Score Sheet* to record its answer. You can use the quarter *Answer Keys* to check your answers and to calculate your final scores.

1

The *Player / Team Score Sheets* have been designed so that each team can answer all questions or you can divide the questions up in any combination you would prefer. For example, you may want to alternate questions if two players are playing or answer every third question for three players, etc. In any case, simply record your response to your questions in the corresponding quarter and question number on the *Player / Team Score Sheet*.

A winner will be determined by multiplying the total number of correct answers for each quarter by the point value per quarter, then adding together the final total for all quarters combined. Play the game again and again by alternating the questions that your team is assigned so that you will answer a different set of questions each time you play.

You Create the Game -
There are countless other ways of using **Nittany Lionology Trivia Challenge** questions. It's limited only to your imagination. Examples might be using them at your tailgate or other college football related party. Players / Teams who answer questions incorrectly may have to perform a required action, or winners may receive special prizes. Let us know what other games you come up with!

Have fun!

NITTANY LIONOLOGY TRIVIA CHALLENGE

1) What year did Penn State officially adopt the nickname "Nittany Lions" for the school's athletics?

    A) 1890
    B) 1897
    C) 1906
    D) 1910

2) What are the Nittany Lions' official colors?

    A) Blue and White
    B) Navy Blue and Cream
    C) Black and White
    D) Bright White and Midnight Blue

3) Penn State's stadium has a seating capacity exceeding 105,000.

    A) True
    B) False

4) What year did Penn State play its first game?

    A) 1879
    B) 1884
    C) 1887
    D) 1890

5) What is the nickname of the Penn State Marching Band?

    A) Penn State Pride
    B) Beaver Blue
    C) Pride of Nittany
    D) Blue Band

6) Who was Penn State's head coach immediately prior to Joe Paterno?

    A) Joe Bedenk
    B) Sam Boyle
    C) Rip Engle
    D) Pop Golden

7) What is the name of the Penn State fight song?

    A) Fight On, State
    B) Victors
    C) Big Blue
    D) Gladiators of the East

8) Which Nittany Lions head coach had the longest tenure?

    A) Joe Paterno
    B) Rip Engle
    C) Hugo Bezdek
    D) Dick Harlow

9) Who was the first player from Penn State to be picked number one in the NFL Draft?

    A) Lenny Moore
    B) Blair Thomas
    C) Curt Warner
    D) Ki-Jana Carter

10) What trophy is awarded to the winner of the annual Penn State-Michigan State matchup?

    A) Paul Bunyan Trophy
    B) Land Grant Trophy
    C) Governor's Cup
    D) Roosevelt Award

11) How many Heisman Trophies have been won by Penn State players?

    A) 1
    B) 2
    C) 3
    D) 5

12) Do the Nittany Lions have a winning record against Ohio State?

    A) Yes
    B) No

13) What is the name of Penn State's costumed mascot?

A) Tony
B) Nittany Lion
C) Ray
D) Chomps

14) What nickname has the PSU football program earned over the years?

A) Tailback U
B) Iron Curtain
C) Linebacker U
D) Blue Blitzers

15) What is the name of the stadium where the Nittany Lions play?

A) Commonwealth Field
B) Beaver Stadium
C) Nittany Field
D) Pennsylvania Field

16) In which year was the first undefeated season for Penn State (min. 8 games)?

A) 1911
B) 1920
C) 1927
D) 1932

17) What color scarf does Penn State's costumed mascot wear?

    A) Blue
    B) White
    C) Blue and White Stripes
    D) Black and White Stripes

18) What is the name of the pre-game pep rally that takes place at the Bryce Jordan Center before home games?

    A) Lion's Roar
    B) Blue Shout
    C) Nittany Roar
    D) Tailgreat

19) Who holds the Penn State career rushing record?

    A) Tony Hunt
    B) Larry Johnson
    C) Curt Warner
    D) Booker Moore

20) As a team, did the Nittany Lions pass for more 2,500 yards in 2007?

    A) Yes
    B) No

21) In 2007, how many touchdown drives did Penn State have of 80 or more yards?

    A) 4
    B) 5
    C) 7
    D) 9

22) What is the name of Penn State's indoor practice facility?

    A) Holuba Hall
    B) Lasch Football Complex
    C) Pennypacker Hall
    D) University Club

23) Since 1900, half of Penn State's wins have been under Joe Paterno.

    A) True
    B) False

24) What year did Penn State begin playing football in the Big Ten?

    A) 1982
    B) 1989
    C) 1990
    D) 1993

25) Who holds the record for passing yards in a single game at Penn State?

    A) Zack Mills
    B) Kerry Collins
    C) Todd Blackledge
    D) Wally Richardson

26) What song does Old Main chime on football Saturday?

    A) Victory
    B) Fight On, State
    C) Penn State Alma Mater
    D) The Nittany Lion

27) Do the Nittany Lions have a losing record against any U.S. Service Academy?

    A) Yes
    B) No

28) When was the last time PSU lost a homecoming game?

    A) 1998
    B) 2000
    C) 2004
    D) 2007

First Quarter

29) Has any Penn State quarterback gained over 1,500 yards rushing and 3,500 yards passing in a career?

    A) Yes
    B) No

30) Who holds the Penn State record for total yards in a single game against Michigan State?

    A) Larry Johnson
    B) Rashard Casey
    C) Bobby Engram
    D) Kerry Collins

31) Who led the Nittany Lions in sacks in 2007?

    A) Tyrell Sales
    B) Dan Connor
    C) Maurice Evans
    D) Chris Baker

32) Which team has Penn State played LESS THAN three times in a bowl game?

    A) Alabama
    B) Tennessee
    C) Florida State
    D) Southern Cal

33) Who is the only Penn State player to win the Biletnikoff Award?

- A) Bobby Engram
- B) Kenny Jackson
- C) Freddie Scott
- D) Chafie Fields

34) Which team was the last opponent Penn State tied?

- A) West Virginia
- B) Syracuse
- C) Maryland
- D) Cincinnati

35) When was the last time Penn State had two First Team Academic All-Americans?

- A) 1987
- B) 1994
- C) 2000
- D) 2006

36) Has PSU ever had a three-time All-American?

- A) Yes
- B) No

37) What was Lenny Moore's nickname while playing at Penn State?

  A) Reading Rambler
  B) Train Wreck
  C) Locomotion
  D) Rough Railer

38) For all games played in 2007, which quarter did the Nittany Lions score the most points?

  A) First
  B) Second
  C) Third
  D) Fourth

39) In the lyrics of the Penn State fight song, what do "we predict"?

  A) Score
  B) Touchdown
  C) Victory
  D) Win

40) When was "The Lion Shrine" unveiled at PSU?

  A) 1940
  B) 1942
  C) 1950
  D) 1953

41) How many *AP* National Championships has Penn State been awarded?

- A) 1
- B) 2
- C) 3
- D) 5

42) Who holds the Penn State record for receiving yards in a season?

- A) Bobby Engram
- B) Deon Butler
- C) Freddie Scott
- D) Mickey Shuler

43) Who is the play-by-play announcer for the Penn State Sports Network?

- A) Roger Corey
- B) Guy Junker
- C) Jack Ham
- D) Steve Jones

44) How many Big Ten Championships has Penn State won?

- A) 1
- B) 2
- C) 3
- D) 5

First Quarter

45) Which player holds the single game rushing record at Penn State?

    A) Curt Warner
    B) Curtis Enis
    C) Larry Johnson
    D) Ki-Jana Carter

46) Who was the opponent in Penn State's last overtime game?

    A) Minnesota
    B) Florida State
    C) Illinois
    D) Northwestern

47) How many PSU head coaches lasted one season or less?

    A) 2
    B) 4
    C) 5
    D) 7

48) What award did Penn State Linebacker Dan Connor win in 2007?

    A) Butkus Award
    B) Lombardi Award
    C) Outland Trophy
    D) Bednarik Award

49) Who holds the Penn State career record for points scored?

- A) Lydell Mitchell
- B) Travis Forney
- C) Craig Fayak
- D) Kevin Kelly

50) Against which Big Ten opponent does Penn State have the best conference record?

- A) Indiana
- B) Michigan State
- C) Illinois
- D) Wisconsin

First Quarter Nittany Lion Cool Fact

One of the wildest finishes in Penn State Bowl history came in the 1969 Orange Bowl against Kansas. The Nittany Lions entered the game undefeated and ranked 3rd in the *AP* Poll. The Jayhawks had one loss and were ranked 6th. Kansas took a 14-7 lead early in the fourth quarter. With less than two minutes left in the game it was announced that Kansas running back Donnie Shanklin was named the Outstanding Performer of the game. Penn State blocked a punt with 1:16 remaining and drove to score. Paterno decided to go for the win instead of the tie and the Jayhawks held. As Kansas fans began to celebrate, the officials threw a flag for 12 men on the field. Paterno went for two again and the Nittany Lions were successful. Afterwards, game film showed that the Jayhawks actually had 12 men on the field for four consecutive plays.

First Quarter Answer Key

1) C – 1906 (The mountain lion that once roamed the Nittany Valley was chosen as the school's mascot by the student body.)

2) A – Blue and White (These colors became official in 1890.)

3) A – True (The current stadium capacity is 107,282 giving Penn State the second largest college football stadium in the country.)

4) C – 1887 (Penn State defeated Bucknell 54-0 in their first football game.)

5) D – Blue Band (In 1923, a few members replaced their brown uniforms with new blue uniforms and shortly after the band became known as the Blue Band.)

6) C – Rip Engle (He coached the Nittany Lions for 16 years from 1950-65.)

7) A – Fight On, State (The song is played during pre-game and after each PSU score.)

8) A – Joe Paterno (43 years, 1966-current)

9) D – Ki-Jana Carter (He was picked number one overall by the Cincinnati Bengals in the 1995 NFL Draft.)

10) B – Land Grant Trophy (This trophy was first awarded in 1993 and honors the schools as the first land-grant universities. Both schools were founded in February of 1855. PSU is 11-4 in the trophy game.)

11) A – 1 (John Cappelletti won the award in 1973 after rushing for 1,522 yards and 17 touchdowns.)

12) B – No (Penn State has an overall record of 11-12 against the Buckeyes for a .478 winning percentage.)

13) B – Nittany Lion (Nittany Lion has added entertainment to football games since first appearing in 1922.)

14) C – Linebacker U (There have been 14 Penn State linebackers named All-American a total of 18 times since 1968.)

15) B – Beaver Stadium (Opened in 1960 with an original seating capacity of 46,284)

16) A – 1911 (The Nittany Lions finished 8-0-1.)

17) C – Blue and White Stripes (This is the only accessory worn by the costumed Nittany Lion [aside from the traditional black Nikes].)

18) D – Tailgreat (The Blue Band performs its pregame and halftime music with appearances by the cheerleaders and Nittany Lion.)

19) C – Curt Warner (He gained 3,398 rushing yards on 649 carries for 24 touchdowns from 1979-82.)

20) A – Yes (The Nittany Lions completed 240 passes on 415 attempts for 2,682 yards.)

21) B – 5 (One against Temple, Indiana & Iowa and two against Texas A&M)

22) A – Holuba Hall (Located within the Lasch Football Complex, Holuba Hall is over 118,000 square feet and contains two 80-yard indoor football fields.)

23) B – False (Penn State has won 756 games since 1900, of which 372 [49.2%] have been under Joe Paterno.)

24) D – 1993 (Penn State was voted a member of the Big Ten in 1990 but did not participate in football until 1993.)

25) A – Zack Mills (He threw for 399 yards against Iowa in 2002.)

26) D – The Nittany Lion (During the week Westminster Quarters is chimed, but it is switched to The Nittany Lion for the weekend.)

27) B – No (Penn State is 3-0 against Air Force, 13-10-2 against Army and 18-17-2 against Navy for a combined record of 34-27-4 [.554].)

28) C – 2004 (Penn State lost 4-6 to Iowa. PSU holds a 63-20-5 all-time homecoming record for a .744 winning percentage.)

29) A – Yes (Michael Robinson gained 1,637 yards rushing and 3,531 yards passing from 2002-05.)

30) D – Kerry Collins (He passed for 352 yards with -2 yards rushing for 350 yards of total offense against the Spartans in 1993 [PSU 38, MSU 37].)

31) C – Maurice Evans (He led the team with 12.5 sacks for -94 yards.)

32) D – Southern Cal (Penn State has played USC twice in bowl games and all other teams listed a total of three times each.)

33) A – Bobby Engram (He won this award, which is given to the nation's best wide receiver, in 1995.)

34) C – Maryland (Penn State played to a 13-13 tie with the Terrapins in 1989.)

35) D – 2006 (Paul Posluszny and Tim Shaw made First Team Academic All-American. Nolan McCready was named Second Team.)

36) B – No (Although there have been many 2-time All-Americans, no player has been named 3-time All-American.)

37) A – Reading Rambler (Moore was 6', 185 lbs and had a career average of 6.2 yards per carry from 1953-55. Paterno has said Moore was the best player he had ever seen.)

38) B – Second (PSU scored a total of 131 points in the second quarter while only allowing 21 points.)

39) C – Victory ("Victory we predict for thee.")

40) B – 1942 (The shrine was dedicated by the Class of 1940 and was carved from a 13-ton block of limestone.)

41) B – 2 (1982 and 1986)

42) A – Bobby Engram (He set the record in 1995 with
       1,084 yards in 63 receptions.)

43) D – Steve Jones (He has teamed up with color analyst
       Jack Ham since 2000.)

44) B – 2 (PSU won the Big Ten in 1994 and 2005.)

45) C – Larry Johnson (He rushed for 327 yards against
       Indiana in 2002.)

46) A – Minnesota (PSU beat the Golden Gophers 28-27 in
       2006. Minnesota scored in the first overtime but the
       extra point hit the upright. Penn State scored and
       the extra point split the uprights for the win.)

47) B – 4 (Sam Boyle [1899], Dan Reed [1903], Jack
       Hollenback [1910], and Joe Bedenk [1949])

48) D – Bednarik Award (Given to the Defensive Player of
       the Year by the Maxwell Football Club of
       Philadelphia since 1993, Connor became the third
       Penn State player to receive the award.)

49) D – Kevin Kelly (305 points scored from 2005-07 [123
       extra points, 58 field goals, and 1 touchdown])

50) A – Indiana (Penn State is a perfect 11-0 against the
       Hoosiers in Big Ten play.)

Note: All answers valid as of the end of the 2007
season, unless otherwise indicated in the question
itself.

NITTANY LIONOLOGY TRIVIA CHALLENGE

1) How many students make up the "Block S" in the stands at Beaver Stadium?

- A) 500
- B) 700
- C) 850
- D) One for every all-time win

2) How many times has Penn State finished the season undefeated (minimum 5 games)?

- A) 7
- B) 8
- C) 10
- D) 12

3) How many PSU defensive players are in the College Football Hall of Fame?

- A) 1
- B) 3
- C) 4
- D) 6

4) How many different decades have the Nittany Lions won at least 85 games?

- A) 1
- B) 2
- C) 3
- D) 5

5) Was Penn State penalized for 100 or more yards in any game in 2007?

    A) Yes
    B) No

6) What number did John Cappelletti wear?

    A) 22
    B) 25
    C) 29
    D) 32

7) When was the first time the Nittany Lions traveled out-of-state for a game?

    A) 1887
    B) 1890
    C) 1893
    D) 1900

8) How many years did Penn State play without a head coach?

    A) 2
    B) 5
    C) 6
    D) 8

9) Has Penn State ever lost a game when scoring 50+ points?

    A) Yes
    B) No

10) Who led Penn State in interceptions in 2007?

    A) Anthony Scirrotto
    B) Justin King
    C) Tony Davis
    D) Lydell Sargeant

11) How many unanswered points did PSU score against Pittsburgh in 1981?

    A) 28
    B) 35
    C) 42
    D) 48

12) Which team gained the most total yards ever against PSU in a single game?

    A) Wisconsin
    B) Nebraska
    C) Michigan State
    D) Boston College

13) How many times has Penn State hosted ESPN's *College Gameday*?

    A) 4
    B) 6
    C) 10
    D) 13

14) When was the last time a player gained 200 or more rushing yards in a single game against Penn State?

    A) 1999
    B) 2001
    C) 2003
    D) 2006

15) Who scored the first touchdown for Penn State in the 2007 Alamo Bowl?

    A) Deon Butler
    B) Daryll Clark
    C) Evan Royster
    D) Rodney Kinlaw

16) Against which opponent did Anthony Morelli have the best passing efficiency in 2007?

    A) Temple
    B) Indiana
    C) Buffalo
    D) Illinois

Second Quarter *2-Point Questions*

17) What is the Penn State record for fewest total yards allowed in a single game?

    A) -47
    B) -6
    C) 2
    D) 8

18) What is the longest winning streak in the Penn State-Ohio State series?

    A) 2 games
    B) 4 games
    C) 5 games
    D) 6 games

19) How many Penn State players have been picked number one overall in the NFL Draft?

    A) 1
    B) 2
    C) 4
    D) 5

20) The Nittany Lions have won more than 25 bowl games.

    A) True
    B) False

21) How many yards was the longest rushing play in Penn State history?

    A) 89
    B) 92
    C) 95
    D) 99

22) In which bowl was Penn State's first bowl appearance?

    A) Cotton Bowl
    B) Gator Bowl
    C) Rose Bowl
    D) Sugar Bowl

23) How many Penn State players are in the CoSIDA Academic Hall of Fame?

    A) 1
    B) 2
    C) 4
    D) 5

24) How many tackles for loss did the Nittany Lions record in 2007?

    A) 68
    B) 79
    C) 85
    D) 102

Second Quarter

25) Who was named MVP for Penn State in the 1995 Rose Bowl?

    A) Kyle Brady
    B) Bobby Engram
    C) Kerry Collins
    D) Ki-Jana Carter

26) How many times have the Nittany Lions begun the season ranked #1 in the first *AP* Poll?

    A) 1
    B) 2
    C) 4
    D) 5

27) How many times has PSU gone undefeated/untied and not been awarded an *AP* National Championship?

    A) 1
    B) 2
    C) 4
    D) 5

28) Who is the only Penn State player to be twice awarded Outstanding Offensive Player of the Fiesta Bowl?

    A) Curt Warner
    B) Todd Blackledge
    C) D.J. Dozier
    D) O.J. McDuffie

Second Quarter *2-Point Questions*

29) Who was the first head coach at Penn State?

- A) Samuel Newton
- B) George Hoskins
- C) Pop Golden
- D) Tom Fennell

30) How many games did Penn State play in its first season?

- A) 2
- B) 3
- C) 5
- D) 6

31) In 2007, how many times did a Penn State player gain over 100 yards receiving?

- A) 1
- B) 3
- C) 4
- D) 6

32) Against which BCS Conference does Penn State have the best winning percentage?

- A) SEC
- B) ACC
- C) Pac 10
- D) Big East

Second Quarter *2-Point Questions*

33) Who holds the Penn State freshman rushing record?

    A) Curtis Enis
    B) Curt Warner
    C) D.J. Dozier
    D) Lenny Moore

34) What is the Penn State record for most consecutive Big Ten losses?

    A) 3
    B) 4
    C) 6
    D) 7

35) To which team did Penn State suffer its worst loss ever?

    A) Lehigh
    B) Harvard
    C) Alabama
    D) Oregon State

36) Who was Penn State's first opponent in Beaver Stadium?

    A) Pittsburgh
    B) Syracuse
    C) Boston University
    D) Virginia Tech

Second Quarter *2-Point Questions*

37) What nickname has Penn State home games earned over recent years?

- A) Lions Claw
- B) Blue Pride
- C) White Out
- D) Screaming Valley

38) Which player set the PSU record for most rushing yards AGAINST the Nittany Lions in a single game?

- A) Tyrone Wheatley
- B) Ted Brown
- C) Tony Dorsett
- D) Chris Wells

39) Who holds the Penn State record for passing yards in a season?

- A) Todd Blackledge
- B) Kerry Collins
- C) Zack Mills
- D) Mike MxQueary

40) Penn State has never given up 500 points in a single season.

- A) True
- B) False

41) Who holds the PSU record for most receiving yards in a single game?

- A) Bryant Johnson
- B) Bobby Engram
- C) Joe Jurevicius
- D) Deon Butler

42) How many PSU players have had over 1,000 yards receiving in a single season?

- A) 1
- B) 2
- C) 4
- D) 5

43) Who is the only Penn State player to be named Big Ten Freshman of the Year?

- A) Curtis Enis
- B) Michael Robinson
- C) Derrick Williams
- D) Courtney Brown

44) Was Penn State the outright Big Ten Champion in 1994 and 2005?

- A) Yes
- B) No

45) What is located in the southwest corner of Beaver Stadium?

    A) Penn State Football Hall of Fame
    B) Walk of Fame
    C) Penn State All-Sports Museum
    D) Football History Theater

46) Has any Nittany Lion ever had 20 or more career interceptions?

    A) Yes
    B) No

47) What is the Penn State record for consecutive non-losing seasons (includes .500 seasons)?

    A) 28
    B) 34
    C) 41
    D) 49

48) What year was Joe Paterno awarded the Amos Alonzo Stagg Award?

    A) 1977
    B) 1982
    C) 1994
    D) 2002

Second Quarter *2-Point Questions*

49) Which decade did Penn State have the best winning percentage?

   A) 1940s
   B) 1960s
   C) 1970s
   D) 1990s

50) What "lucky charm" did the Nittany Lions carry with them in 1968?

   A)   Bamboo horseshoe
   B)   Rabbits foot
   C)   Rip Engle's hat
   D)   Broken PSU helmet

Second Quarter Nittany Lion Cool Fact

In 1928, a group of Penn State fans began gathering at the Nittany Lion Inn to discuss previous games and the team's upcoming opponent. The group soon became known as the State College Quarterback Club. The club currently meets every Wednesday at the Mount Nittany Club inside Beaver Stadium. Joe Paterno joins the meetings on a regular basis and will occasionally bring players along. The club is open to all fans and gives members the opportunity to meet those inside the football program.

Second Quarter Answer Key

1) B – 700 (This tradition was revived in 1999 by the Penn State Lion Ambassadors. Students mark seats on Friday night to coordinate the t-shirt color needed for each seat.)

2) D – 12 (1894, 1909, 1911, 1912, 1920, 1921, 1947, 1968, 1969, 1973, 1986, and 1994)

3) B – 3 (Jack Ham [linebacker], Dennis Onkotz [linebacker], and Mike Reid [defensive tackle])

4) C – 3 (PSU won 96 games during the '70s, 89 games during the '80s, and 97 games during the '90s.)

5) B – No (88 yards against Purdue was the highest single game total.)

6) A – 22 (John lettered for the Nittany Lions from 1971-73.)

7) C – 1893 (The Nittany Lions beat the Virginia Cavaliers 6-0 in Penn State's first out-of-state game.)

8) B – 5 (The Nittany Lions played without a head coach from 1887-91 and went 12-8-1 during that period for a .595 winning percentage.)

9) B – No (Penn State has scored 50 or more points 79 times and is undefeated in those games.)

10) A – Anthony Scirrotto (He led the team with 3 interceptions [Buffalo, Wisconsin, and Michigan State].)

11) D – 48 (The Nittany Lions fell behind 0-14 in the first quarter to the top-ranked Panthers led by Dan Marino. Penn State scored 48 unanswered against the #1 defense in the country [PSU 48, Pitt 14].)

12) D – Boston College (The Eagles gained 656 yards against PSU in 1982 [PSU 52, BC 17].)

13) A – 4 (Beaver Stadium has been the site for four games. Penn State has been one of the two teams a total of ten times.)

14) C – 2003 (BenJarvus Green-Ellis from Indiana gained 203 yards against the Nittany Lions in 2003. Only 10 players have ever gained 200 or more rushing yards in a single game against Penn State.)

15) A – Deon Butler (He scored in the second quarter on a 30-yard touchdown pass from Anthony Morelli.)

16) C – Buffalo (He completed 20 of 27 passes for 202 yards and 4 touchdowns with no interceptions for an efficiency rating of 185.8.)

17) A – -47 (Penn State held Syracuse to -107 yards rushing and 60 yards passing [PSU 40, Syracuse 0].)

18) B – 4 games (PSU beat the Buckeyes their first four meetings [1912, 1956, 1963, and 1964].)

19) B – 2 (Ki-Jana Carter to the Bengals in 1995 and Courtney Brown to the Cleveland Browns in 2000.)

20) A – True (Penn State has won 26 bowl games. Only Alabama [31] and Southern Cal [30] have won more.)

21) B – 92 (Blair Thomas set this record against Syracuse in 1986.)

22) C – Rose Bowl (Penn State lost 3-14 to Southern Cal in the 1923 Rose Bowl.)

23) B – 2 (Todd Blackledge was inducted in 1997 and David Joyner was inducted in 1991.)

24) D – 102 (Overall, the tackles combined for -439 yards. Maurice Evans led the team with 21.5.)

25) D – Ki-Jana Carter (He carried the ball 21 times for 156 yards and three touchdowns [PSU 38, Oregon 20].)

26) A – 1 (Penn State started at #1 in 1997 and finished 16th in the last poll after a 9-3 season.)

27) C – 4 (Penn State went undefeated in 1968 [Ohio State awarded *AP* Title], 1969 [Texas], 1973 [Notre Dame], and 1994 [Nebraska].)

28) A – Curt Warner (He was given this award for his performance in the 1980 and 1982 Fiesta Bowls.)

29) B – George Hoskins (He coached PSU from 1892-95 and played center on the team from 1892-94.)

30) A – 2 (Penn State played Bucknell twice, winning the first matchup 24-0 and the second 54-0.)

31) A – 1 (Derrick Williams gained 104 yards receiving on seven catches against Temple [PSU 31, Temple 0].)

32) B – ACC (The Nittany Lions have an all-time record of 89-21-2 against the ACC for a .804 winning percentage.)

33) C – D.J. Dozier (He rushed for 1,002 yards in 1983. He went on to gain 3,227 career yards from 1983-86.)

34) D – 7 (Penn State lost the last Big Ten game in 2003 and the first six of the 2004 season.)

35) A – Lehigh (The Nittany Lions fell 0-106 to the Mountain Hawks in 1889.)

36) C – Boston University (The Nittany Lions beat the Terriers 20-0.)

37) C – White Out (Fans are encouraged to wear white t-shirts to cheer on the Nittany Lions.)

38) B – Ted Brown (He gained 251 rushing yards against Penn State in 1977 [PSU 21, NC State 17].)

39) B – Kerry Collins (He completed 176 of 264 passes for 2,679 yards in 1994.)

40) A – True (The most points the Nittany Lions have given up in a season were 312 points in 1983.)

41) D – Deon Butler (In 2006 he gained 216 yards against Northwestern [PSU 33, NW 7].)

42) A – 1 (Bobby Engram had 1,029 yards in 1994 & 1,084 yards in 1995 and is the only Nittany Lion to surpass the 1,000 yard receiving mark.)

43) A – Curtis Enis (He was voted Freshman of the Year by the media in 1995.)

44) B – No (PSU was the outright Champion in 1994 but shared the title with Ohio State in 2005 even though the Nittany Lions beat the Buckeyes 17-10.)

45) C – Penn State All-Sports Museum (The 10,000 square foot museum opened in 2002 and honors all of Penn State's athletic programs.)

46) B – No (Neal Smith came the closest with 19 interceptions from 1967-69.)

47) D – 49 (Penn State did not have a losing season from 1939-87. The Nittany Lions went 5-6 in 1988.)

48) D – 2002 (This award is voted on by the American Football Coaches Association and is given to those who have advanced the best interest of football.)

49) C – 1970s (Penn State had an overall record of 96-22 during the '70s for a .814 winning percentage.)

50) A – Bamboo horseshoe (Found following a victory over Navy, the team carried the horseshoe with them all season on their way to an 11-0 record.)

Note: All answers valid as of the end of the 2007 season, unless otherwise indicated in the question itself.

1) How many times has a number-one ranked Penn State team lost in a bowl game?

    A) 1
    B) 2
    C) 3
    D) 4

2) What is the Penn State record for most tackles in a single game?

    A) 21
    B) 24
    C) 26
    D) 29

3) In which year was the first 10-win season at Penn State?

    A) 1947
    B) 1955
    C) 1961
    D) 1968

4) Which PSU head coach has the second highest total wins in team history?

    A) Rip Engle
    B) Bob Higgins
    C) Hugo Bezdek
    D) Dick Harlow

5) What was the largest margin of victory for Penn State in a bowl game?

    A) 24
    B) 29
    C) 33
    D) 38

6) Who holds the PSU career record for receiving yards?

    A) Bryant Johnson
    B) Kyle Brady
    C) Terry Smith
    D) Bobby Engram

7) Which of the following Penn State QBs NEVER threw more than 20 touchdown passes in a single season?

    A) Todd Blackledge
    B) Kerry Collins
    C) Zack Mills
    D) Tony Sacca

8) How many combined kickoffs and punts were returned for touchdowns by the Nittany Lions in 2007?

    A) 0
    B) 2
    C) 3
    D) 4

9) Who is the only Penn State player to kick a field goal of 55 or more yards?

    A) Kevin Kelly
    B) Brett Conway
    C) Craig Fayak
    D) Chris Bahr

10) Which award has been won the most number of times by Penn State players?

    A) Butkus Award
    B) Walter Camp Award
    C) Maxwell Award
    D) Davey O'Brien Award

11) Penn State surpassed 800 all-time victories in 2007.

    A) True
    B) False

12) How many games did Kerry Collins pass for more than 200 yards in 1994?

    A) 7
    B) 8
    C) 10
    D) 11

13) What is the Penn State record for most sacks in a season?

    A)   13.5
    B)   15.0
    C)   16.0
    D)   17.5

14) Has any Penn State player ever had 100+ yards rushing and 100+ yards receiving in the same game?

    A)   Yes
    B)   No

15) Which coach has the best winning percentage at PSU?

    A)   George Hoskins
    B)   Joe Paterno
    C)   Rip Engle
    D)   Bill Hollenback

16) When was the last time a kickoff was returned 100 yards for a touchdown by a Penn State returner?

    A)   1975
    B)   1986
    C)   1994
    D)   2001

Third Quarter   *3-Point Questions*

17) Who was the last Penn State player to record over 75 solo tackles in a single season?

    A) Paul Posluszny
    B) Brandon Short
    C) Shawn Mayer
    D) Greg Buttle

18) What is the PSU record for most rushing yards against a Big Ten opponent?

    A) 246
    B) 261
    C) 284
    D) 327

19) When was the last time the season leading passer for Penn State had less than 1,000 yards passing?

    A) 1988
    B) 1991
    C) 1998
    D) 2002

20) Who was the last Penn State quarterback to throw five touchdowns in a single game?

    A) Zack Mills
    B) Anthony Morelli
    C) Michael Robinson
    D) Rashard Casey

Third Quarter

3-Point Questions

21) Penn State has won more than 80% of its home games.

    A) True
    B) False

22) How many Penn State head coaches have also been named All-American as a Nittany Lion?

    A) 1
    B) 2
    C) 4
    D) 5

23) For which bowl game victory was a Penn State player not voted MVP?

    A) 1989 Holiday Bowl
    B) 1996 Outback Bowl
    C) 2006 Fiesta Bowl
    D) 2007 Outback Bowl

24) How many Penn State players had 25 or more receptions in 2007?

    A) 1
    B) 2
    C) 4
    D) 5

25) All-time, how many weeks has Penn State been ranked #1 in the *AP* Poll?

    A) 19
    B) 23
    C) 30
    D) 36

26) Who was the first All-American linebacker at Penn State?

    A) Jack Ham
    B) Dennis Onkotz
    C) John Skorupan
    D) Ed O'Neil

27) Has Penn State ever allowed two different players to rush for 200+ yards against them in a single game?

    A) Yes
    B) No

28) Who was the last Penn State player to record 10 or more receiving touchdowns in a single season?

    A) O.J. McDuffie
    B) Kenny Jackson
    C) Bobby Engram
    D) Joe Jurevicius

Third Quarter

29) How many Penn State players have been named All-American more than once?

    A) 10
    B) 12
    C) 14
    D) 16

30) What was the combined winning percentage of coaches who lasted one season or less at Penn State?

    A) .556
    B) .627
    C) .791
    D) .823

31) Against which team did PSU get their first Big Ten win?

    A) Northwestern
    B) Iowa
    C) Minnesota
    D) Purdue

32) What is Penn State's longest drought between bowl games since 1960?

    A) 3 years
    B) 4 years
    C) 6 years
    D) 7 years

Third Quarter

3-Point Questions

NITTANY LIONOLOGY TRIVIA CHALLENGE

33) How many times has Penn State won the Lambert-Meadowlands Trophy?

A) 18
B) 21
C) 26
D) 30

34) Which Nittany Lion had the highest tackle total in a single game in 2007?

A) Maurice Evans
B) Lydell Sargeant
C) Sean Lee
D) Dan Connor

35) Has Penn State ever had two players rush for over 1,000 yards in the same season?

A) Yes
B) No

36) Who holds the Penn State rushing record for consecutive regular season 100 yard games?

A) Curtis Enis
B) Ki-Jana Carter
C) Blair Thomas
D) Matt Suhey

PENN STATE NITTANY LIONS FOOTBALL

Third Quarter   *3-Point Questions*

37) In which year did PSU set its record for most players selected in the first round of the NFL Draft?

- A) 1974
- B) 1986
- C) 1995
- D) 2003

38) Who is the last Nittany Lion to lead the team in rushing and receiving in the same year?

- A) Tony Hunt
- B) Blair Thomas
- C) Gary Brown
- D) Matt Suhey

39) What were the original chosen colors for Penn State?

- A) Orange and Black
- B) Crimson and Cream
- C) Gold and Gray
- D) Pink and Black

40) When was the last time the leading rusher for Penn State gained less than 500 yards for the season?

- A) 1988
- B) 1992
- C) 1997
- D) 2003

Third Quarter

41) How many Nittany Lions have finished second or third in Heisman voting?

- A) 2
- B) 3
- C) 4
- D) 6

42) How many Penn State players have been drafted in the first round of the NFL Draft?

- A) 28
- B) 31
- C) 34
- D) 42

43) What position did Coach Paterno play in college?

- A) Tight end
- B) Receiver
- C) Cornerback
- D) Linebacker

44) In which of the following categories did the 1947 Nittany Lions NOT lead the nation?

- A) Rushing yards allowed per game
- B) Passing yards allowed per game
- C) Total yards allowed per game
- D) Points allowed per game

45) What trophy is awarded to the winner of the Penn State-Minnesota game?

A) Iroquois Spear
B) Governor's Trophy
C) Bronze Bridge Award
D) Governor's Victory Bell

46) Penn State has never allowed an opposing quarterback to throw for more than 500 yards in a single game.

A) True
B) False

47) Where did the Nittany Lions play before Beaver Stadium?

A) New Beaver Field
B) Carnegie Field
C) Penn Stadium
D) Eisenhower Field

48) In 2007, how many teams did Penn State hold to fewer than 100 yards rushing?

A) 5
B) 6
C) 8
D) 10

49) As a team, did Penn State have a net gain of more than 2,500 rushing yards in 2007?

    A) Yes
    B) No

50) What are the most consecutive bowl losses by the Nittany Lions?

    A) 1
    B) 2
    C) 3
    D) 5

Third Quarter Nittany Lion Cool Fact

The 1987 Fiesta Bowl matched up #1 Miami against #2 Penn State. Before this game, the four major bowl games (Rose, Orange, Sugar, and Cotton) had affiliations with the major conferences. Since Penn State and Miami were independents at the time, the Fiesta Bowl was able to court both teams to play for the national championship. This was the first bowl game ever to have a title sponsorship. Sunkist would benefit from the hype created by the chemistry of the two contrasting teams involved. Miami players walked with a cocky swagger rarely, if ever, seen in college football up to that point. Penn State players approached each game in a business-like fashion and were coached to believe that no player was more important than the team. The drama played out both before and during the game. Penn State ended up on top even though the Nittany Lions were outgained by 283 yards. The game had a television rating of 25.1 (over 70 million viewers), still ranking as the highest rated college football game in history.

Third Quarter Answer Key

1) B – 2 (Penn State fell 7-14 to #2 Alabama in the 1979 Sugar Bowl and 10-25 to #3 Oklahoma in the 1986 Orange Bowl.)

2) B – 24 (This record is held by two players, Greg Buttle against West Virginia in 1974 and Bill Banks against North Carolina in 1977.)

3) D – 1968 (Penn State finished a perfect 11-0.)

4) A – Rip Engle (104 wins from 1950-65)

5) B – 29 (PSU beat Oregon 41-12 in the 1960 Liberty Bowl and Auburn 43-14 in the 1996 Outback Bowl.)

6) D – Bobby Engram (He had 167 catches for 3,026 yards during his career [1991, 1993-95].)

7) C – Zack Mills (His highest season total was 17 in 2002.)

8) B – 2 (Derrick Williams returned a punt 79 yards against Notre Dame and A.J. Wallace returned a kickoff 97 yards against Ohio State.)

9) D – Chris Bahr (He kicked three 55-yard field goals in 1975.)

10) C – Maxwell Award (Seven Penn State players have won this award: Rich Lucas in 1959, Glenn Ressler in 1964, Mike Reid in 1969, John Cappelletti in 1973, Chuck Fusina in 1978, Kerry Collins in 1994, and Larry Johnson in 2002.)

11) B – False (Penn State's all-time record is 789-347-41 for a .688 winning percentage. Penn State ranks sixth among the FBS for all-time victories.)

12) C – 10 (Collins passed for 200+ yards against every team except for Iowa and Northwestern.)

13) B – 15.0 (This mark was achieved by Larry Kubin in1979 and Michael Haynes in 2002.)

14) B – No (Curtis Enis came the closest in 1997 with 186 yards rushing and 83 yards receiving against Purdue.)

15) A – George Hoskins (He had a record of 17-4-4 from 1892-95 for a .826 winning percentage.)

16) A – 1975 (PSU players have returned kicks for 100+ yards four times, most recently by Rich Mauti.)

17) C – Shawn Mayer (He recorded 85 in 2002. Gregg Buttle and James Boyd are the only other players to surpass 75 solo tackles in a single season.)

18) D – 327 (Larry Johnson set this record in 2002 against Indiana. He also had four touchdowns on the day [PSU 58, IU 25].)

19) A – 1988 (Tony Sacca led the Nittany Lions with 694 yards passing.)

20) D – Rashard Casey (Louisiana Tech, 2000)

21) A – True (Penn State has an all-time home record of 229-57 for a .801 winning percentage.)

22) B – 2 (Bob Higgin as an end in 1915 and 1919 and Joe Bedenk as a guard in 1923)

23) C – 2006 Fiesta Bowl (Willie Reid of Florida State was named MVP [PSU 26, FSU 23 in OT].)

24) C – 4 (Derrick Williams [55], Deon Butler [47], Jordan Norwood [40], and Terrell Golden [30])

25) A – 19 (The first time PSU held the top spot was in 1978 and the last time was in 1997.)

26) B – Dennis Onkotz (He was named All-American in 1968 and 1969. He led the team in tackles with 71 in 1968 and 97 in 1969.)

27) A – Yes (Marc Renaud [203 yards] and Sedrick Irvin [238 yards] from Michigan State in 1997 [PSU 14, MSU 49])

28) D – Joe Jurevicius (10 TDs in 1997. Bobby Engram is the only other player to do so [11 in 1995 and 13 in 1993])

29) C – 14 (Dan Connor was the last player to be named two-time All-American [2006-07].)

30) A – .556 (One year coaches had a combined record of 19-15-2.)

31) C – Minnesota (The Nittany Lions beat the Golden Gophers 38-20 in 1993 to win their inaugural Big Ten game.)

32) B – 4 years (PSU did not attend a bowl game following the 1963-66 seasons.)

33) C – 26 (This trophy has been awarded to Eastern footballs top team since 1936.)

34) D – Dan Connor (18 tackles against Ohio State)

35) B – No (PSU has had 17 players rush for over 1,000 yards in a season, but never two in the same season.)

36) A – Curtis Enis (He had eight consecutive 100 yard rushing games in 1997.)

37) D – 2003 (Four first round draft picks: Jimmy Kennedy, Michael Haynes, Bryant Johnson, & Larry Johnson.)

38) A – Tony Hunt (In 2006, he led the team with 777 rushing yards and 334 receiving yards. Only four other players have accomplished the same feat [Billy Kane in 1956, Jim Kerr in 1960, D.J. Dozier in 1986, and Blair Thomas in 1987].)

39) D – Pink and Black (A group of students unanimously chose this color combination in 1887. Problems arose when the Pink faded to white after sun exposure, so it was agreed upon three years later to change the colors to the current Blue and White.)

40) D – 2003 (Austin Scott led the Nittany Lions with 436 rushing yards off of 100 carries.)

41) B – 3 (Chuck Fusina finished second in 1978 [Billy Sims won], Ki-Jana Carter finished second in 1994 [Rashaan Salaam won], and Larry Johnson finished third in 2002 [Carson Palmer won].)

42) C – 34 (The last player taken in the first round was Levi Brown in the 2007 NFL Draft.)

43) C – Cornerback (He also played quarterback at Brown.)

44) B – Passing yards allowed per game (The PSU defense allowed a per game average of 3 points, 17 yards rushing, and 76.8 total yards.)

45) D – Governor's Victory Bell (First awarded in 1993 to welcome PSU into the Big Ten as Minnesota was the first conference opponent for Penn State.)

46) B – False (Doug Flutie passed for 520 yards in 1982 and Ty Detmer passed for 576 yards against PSU in the 1989 Holiday Bowl.)

47) A – New Beaver Field (PSU played here from 1909-59. The stadium was dismantled and was used to form the base of the new Beaver Stadium.)

48) C – 8 (Florida International [-3], Notre Dame [0], Buffalo [56], Iowa [48], Wisconsin [87], Indiana [68], Purdue [68], and Temple [4].)

49) A – Yes (PSU had a net gain of 2,519 rushing yards.)

50) B – 2 (6-13 to Alabama in the 1975 Sugar Bowl and 9-20 to Notre Dame in the 1976 Gator Bowl)

Note: All answers valid as of the end of the 2007 season, unless otherwise indicated in the question itself.

Fourth Quarter *4-Point Questions*

1) How many Penn State players are in the College Football Hall of Fame for more than one position?

    A) 1
    B) 2
    C) 3
    D) 5

2) Of the following Ivy League schools, which is the only one the Nittany Lions HAVE beaten?

    A) Harvard
    B) Princeton
    C) Columbia
    D) Brown

3) Who was Penn State's opponent in the game that set the attendance record at Beaver Stadium?

    A) Ohio State
    B) Michigan
    C) Nebraska
    D) Notre Dame

4) The Nittany Lions have never had more than two players gain 100+ rushing yards in the same game.

    A) True
    B) False

5) Which team scored the most points against the Nittany Lions in 2007?

A) Michigan
B) Texas A&M
C) Michigan State
D) Ohio State

6) When was the last time PSU led the nation in total defense?

A) 1978
B) 1983
C) 1986
D) 1992

7) What is the Penn State record for most consecutive seasons appearing in a bowl game?

A) 8
B) 10
C) 13
D) 16

8) How many Penn State coaches are in the College Football Hall of Fame?

A) 2
B) 3
C) 5
D) 6

Fourth Quarter *4-Point Questions*

9) Who is the only Penn State player to lead the team in rushing for four years?

    A) Curt Warner
    B) D.J. Dozier
    C) Curtis Enis
    D) Tony Hunt

10) Who is the only player to lead the Nittany Lions in rushing yards and passing yards in the same season?

    A) Michael Robinson
    B) Rashard Casey
    C) Dayle Tate
    D) Rich Lucas

11) Which Penn State building can be found on the Land Grant Trophy?

    A) Old Main
    B) Beaver Stadium
    C) Hetzel Union
    D) Eisenhower Chapel

12) Which player holds the Penn State record for points scored in a single season?

    A) John Cappelletti
    B) Franco Harris
    C) Lydell Mitchell
    D) Curtis Enis

Fourth Quarter *4-Point Questions*

13) In which offensive category did Penn State lead the Big Ten in 2007?

    A) Rushing
    B) Red zone offense
    C) Third down conversions
    D) First downs

14) Who holds the Penn State single season rushing record?

    A) Curt Warner
    B) Tony Hunt
    C) Eric McCoo
    D) Larry Johnson

15) When was the last time the Nittany Lions were shutout?

    A) 1996
    B) 1999
    C) 2001
    D) 2003

16) Has any Penn State punter ever recorded a punt of 90 or more yards?

    A) Yes
    B) No

Fourth Quarter *4-Point Questions*

17) Who was the first African-American All-American for the Nittany Lions?

    A) Charlie Pittman
    B) Dave Robinson
    C) Randy Crowder
    D) Lydell Mitchell

18) How many times has Penn State beaten a team ranked #1 in the *AP* Poll?

    A) 4
    B) 6
    C) 8
    D) 9

19) What is the Penn State record for most losses in a single season?

    A) 7
    B) 8
    C) 9
    D) 11

20) Who was the last Nittany Lion quarterback to lead the team in passing for four years?

    A) Tony Sacca
    B) Todd Blackledge
    C) Chuck Fusina
    D) Zack Mills

21) How many all-time head coaches has Penn State had?

- A) 14
- B) 17
- C) 20
- D) 22

22) What is the largest margin of victory for Penn State against Ohio State?

- A) 35 points
- B) 38 points
- C) 42 points
- D) 49 points

23) Which coach has the second best all-time winning percentage at Penn State?

- A) Joe Paterno
- B) Rip Engle
- C) Bob Higgins
- D) Dick Harlow

24) Has Penn State played every Pac 10 team at least once?

- A) Yes
- B) No

Fourth Quarter *4-Point Questions*

25) Which of the following is NOT on the Governor's Victory Bell Trophy?

    A)   Medallion of the Big Ten Conference
    B)   Eleven arrows
    C)   The state seals of PA and MN
    D)   PSU and MSU athletic logos

26) Against which BCS Conference does Penn State have the worst winning percentage?

    A)   SEC
    B)   Big East
    C)   Big 12
    D)   Pac 10

27) What year was the first PSU football game televised?

    A)   1955
    B)   1959
    C)   1962
    D)   1966

28) How many Penn State coaches have won Coach of the Year by the American Football Coaches Association?

    A)   1
    B)   2
    C)   3
    D)   4

Fourth Quarter *4-Point Questions*

29) What decade did Penn State have its worst winning percentage?

    A) 1890s
    B) 1910s
    C) 1930s
    D) 1950s

30) Penn State led the nation in fourth down conversions in 2007.

    A) True
    B) False

31) How many Penn State players are in the College Football Hall of Fame?

    A) 14
    B) 16
    C) 19
    D) 23

32) Which is the only Big Ten team Penn State has faced in a bowl game?

    A) Minnesota
    B) Purdue
    C) Illinois
    D) Ohio State

Fourth Quarter   *4-Point Questions*

33) When was the last time the Nittany Lions gave up a safety?

    A) 1997
    B) 2001
    C) 2004
    D) 2007

34) What was the worst defeat Penn State suffered in a bowl game?

    A) 18 points
    B) 25 points
    C) 31 points
    D) 36 points

35) When was the last time Penn State played Pittsburgh?

    A) 1992
    B) 1998
    C) 2000
    D) 2002

36) How many times has Penn State appeared in the Orange/Sugar/Fiesta/Rose bowls combined?

    A) 12
    B) 15
    C) 17
    D) 22

Fourth Quarter *4-Point Questions*

37) How many Penn State players have won the Outland Trophy?

    A) 0
    B) 1
    C) 3
    D) 4

38) How many touchdown passes did Anthony Morelli have in 2007?

    A) 16
    B) 19
    C) 21
    D) 23

39) Which of these Penn State team records is NOT held by their 1994 team?

    A) Total offense in a season
    B) Passing offense in a season
    C) Rushing offense in a season
    D) Points scored in a season

40) Every 300+ yard passing game by a Nittany Lion quarterback has taken place since 1980.

    A) True
    B) False

Fourth Quarter *4-Point Questions*

41) Which round was John Cappelletti taken in the NFL Draft?

  A) First
  B) Third
  C) Fourth
  D) Not Drafted

42) Who is the only PSU player to win the Lombardi Award?

  A) LaVar Arrington
  B) Keith Dorney
  C) Bruce Clark
  D) Sean Farrell

43) Has any Penn State player ever won four or more national awards in a single season?

  A) Yes
  B) No

44) What was the best winning percentage of a Penn State head coach who lasted one season or less?

  A) .688
  B) .729
  C) .853
  D) 1.000

Fourth Quarter *4-Point Questions*

45) When was the last time the Nittany Lions shutout an opponent?

- A) 1998
- B) 2001
- C) 2005
- D) 2007

46) How many Nittany Lions have scored 100 or more points in a single season?

- A) 3
- B) 5
- C) 8
- D) 9

47) How many Penn State players are in the Pro Football Hall of Fame?

- A) 3
- B) 5
- C) 6
- D) 8

48) What is the Penn State record for most consecutive wins without a tie?

- A) 20
- B) 23
- C) 26
- D) 28

49) What is the Penn State record for consecutive Big Ten wins?

   A) 6
   B) 8
   C) 10
   D) 12

50) How many total FBS coaching changes have there been since Joe Paterno began coaching Penn State?

   A) 783
   B) 798
   C) 802
   D) 816

Fourth Quarter Nittany Lion Cool Fact

Mike Reid is one of the most decorated Penn State linemen to put on the Blue and White. He is the only Nittany Lion to win the Outland Trophy and was inducted into the College Football Hall of Fame in 1987. He played five seasons in the NFL and was twice named All-Pro. Although he was very successful playing football, his true passion was music. He won many Country Music Awards for composition and songwriting and was named "Songwriter of the Year" by Cash Box Magazine in 1984 & 1985 and by the Academy of Country Music in 1986. If inducted into the Country Music Hall of Fame, he will become the first person to be inducted into both the College Football and Country Music Halls of Fame.

Fourth Quarter Answer Key

1) A – 1 (Glenn Ressler played for PSU from 1962-64 and was inducted into the College Football Hall of Fame in 2001 as a center and guard.)

2) D – Brown (PSU is 1-0 against the Bears and are 24-51-8 against the Ivy League for a .337 winning percentage. The Nittany Lions have a combined record of 0-17-2 against Columbia, Princeton, Yale, and Harvard.)

3) C – Nebraska (In 2002, Penn State beat the Cornhuskers 40-7 in front of a record 110,753 fans.)

4) B – False (Penn State had three players rush for over 100 yards against Maryland in 1965 [Bill Rettig, Dave McNaughton, & Mike Irwin] and Boston College in 1969 [Franco Harris, Lydell Mitchell, & Charlie Pittman].)

5) D – Ohio State (The Buckeyes scored 37 against PSU.)

6) A – 1978 (Penn State allowed 203.9 yards per game.)

7) C – 13 (Penn State appeared in a bowl game following each season from 1971-83 compiling a 9-4 record during that span.)

8) C – 5 (Hugo Bezdek, Dick Harlow, and Bob Higgins were inducted in 1954. Rip Engle was inducted in 1974. Joe Paterno, Bobby Bowden, and John Gagliardi were selected in 2006 as the first ever active members. Paterno's induction was delayed until 2007 due to injury.)

9) B – D.J. Dozier (He led the team in rushing from 1983-86.)

10) D – Rich Lucas (He led the team in 1959 with 325 rushing yards and 913 passing yards.)

11) A – Old Main (This landmark building is shown along with Michigan State's Beaumont Tower and the PSU & MSU mascots.)

12) C – Lydell Mitchell (He scored 29 touchdowns in 1971 for a total of 174 points.)

13) B – Red zone offense (The Nittany Lions scored 53 times out of 59 red zone possessions [89.8%] with 34 touchdowns and 19 field goals.)

14) D – Larry Johnson (He set the record in 2002 with 271 carries for 2,089 yards and 20 touchdowns. This was also the most yards gained in the FBS.)

15) C – 2001 (PSU was shutout 0-20 by the Wolverines.)

16) B – No (89 yards is the longest punt ever by a Penn State player. This was accomplished by Coop French in 1930 against Iowa.)

17) B – Dave Robinson (He was named All-American in 1962 and went on to play 12 years in the NFL.)

18) A – 4 (PSU beat Pittsburgh 48-14 in 1981, Georgia 27-23 in 1983, Miami 14-10 in 1987, and Notre Dame 24-21 in 1990.)

19) C – 9 (Penn State went 3-9 in 2003. PSU has only had 5 losing seasons under Paterno [1988, 2000, 2001, 2003, and 2004].)

20) D – Zack Mills (He led the team in passing from 2001-04. The only other quarterback to lead the team in passing for four years was Tony Sacca from 1988-91.)

21) A – 14 (Paterno became the 14th head coach in 1966.)

22) D – 49 points (The Nittany Lions routed the Buckeyes 63-14 in 1994.)

23) A – Joe Paterno (Paterno has led PSU to a 372-125-3 record for a .747 winning percentage.)

24) B – No (PSU has yet to play California, Oregon State, or Washington State.)

25) B – Eleven arrows (All other items listed are found on the trophy. PSU leads the trophy series 6-4.)

26) A – SEC (The Nittany Lions are 16-16 all time against the SEC for a .500 winning percentage.)

27) D – 1966 (Penn State lost 10-12 to Syracuse.)

28) A – 1 (Joe Paterno is the only PSU coach to win the award, which was first given in 1935. He has won the award 5 times [1968, 1978, 1982, 1986, & 2002].)

29) C – 1930s (Penn State had a record of 34-41-6 during the '30s for a .457 winning percentage. This is the only decade that PSU went under .500.)

30) B – False (The Nittany Lions were second in the nation behind LSU. Penn State converted 11 of 14 fourth down attempts for a 78.57 success rate.)

31) B – 16 (John Cappelletti, Keith Dorney, Jack Ham, Glenn Killenger, Ted Kwalick, Rich Lucas, Pete Mauthe, Shorty Miller, Lydell Mitchell, Dennis Onkotz, Mike Reid, Glenn Ressler, Dave Robinson, Steve Suhey, Dexter Very, and Harry Wilson.)

32) D – Ohio State (The Nittany Lions beat the Buckeyes 31-19 in the 1980 Fiesta Bowl.)

33) C – 2004 (PSU intentionally ran out of the end zone as time expired to secure a 22-18 win against the Hoosiers.)

34) B – 25 points (Penn State lost 10-35 to Clemson in the 1988 Citrus Bowl.)

35) C – 2000 (The two teams have met four times [1997-2000] since Penn State joined the Big Ten.)

36) C – 17 (Rose Bowl [2], Orange Bowl [5], Sugar Bowl [4], and Fiesta Bowl [6].)

37) B – 1 (Mike Reid was awarded the Outland Trophy in 1969 as a defensive tackle. The trophy is given to the nation's best interior lineman by the Football Writers Association of America.)

38) B – 19 (His efficiency rating was 124.2 for the season.)

39) C – Rushing offense in a season (The 1994 team scored 526 points [47.8 per game], had 2,962 passing yards [246.8 per game], and 5,722 total yards [476.8 per game]. Rushing yards is held by the 1971 PSU team [3,347 yards, 278.9 per game].)

40) B – False (PSU quarterbacks have passed for 300+ yards 11 times and all of them have taken place since 1980 except for one. In 1977, Chuck Fusina passed for 315 yards against NC State [PSU 21, NC State 17].)

41) A – First (He was taken 11th overall by the Rams in the 1974 NFL Draft.)

42) C – Bruce Clark (He won the award, which is given to the nation's best lineman, in 1978.)

43) B – No (Larry Johnson [2002] and John Cappelletti [1973] each won 3 national awards in a single season but no PSU player has ever won 4.)

44) A – .688 (In 1910, Jack Hollenback led Penn State to a 5-2-1 record.)

45) D – 2007 (Penn State shutout Temple 31-0. This was the second shutout of the season for the Nittany Lions.)

46) C – 8 (Lydell Mitchell [174 points in 1971], John Cappelletti [102 points in 1973], Richie Anderson [116 points in 1992], Ki-Jana Carter [138 points in 1994], Curtis Enis [122 points in 1997], Travis Forney [107 points in 1999], Larry Johnson [140 points in 2002], and Kevin Kelly [110 points in 2007].)

47) B – 5 (Jack Ham was inducted in 1988, Franco Harris in 1990, Mike Michalske in 1964, Lenny Moore in 1975, and Mike Munchak in 2001.)

48) B – 23 (Penn State went 11-0 in 1968 & 1969 and won their first game of the 1970 season. The streak was broken by Colorado [PSU 13, Colorado 41].)

49) D – 12 (The Nittany Lions won the last four conference games of 1993 and all eight of 1994.)

50) D – 816 (Since Paterno took over as head coach in 1966, there have been multiple coaching changes at every school in the FBS.)

Note: All answers valid as of the end of the 2007 season, unless otherwise indicated in the question itself.

Overtime Bonus *4-Point Questions*

1) Which coach has the second longest coaching tenure at Penn State?

    A) Bill Hollenback
    B) Rip Engle
    C) Joe Bedenk
    D) Bob Higgins

2) What is the longest winning streak for the Nittany Lions in the Penn State-Michigan State series?

    A) 2
    B) 4
    C) 5
    D) 6

3) Which Penn State quarterback WAS NOT picked in the first round of the NFL Draft?

    A) Todd Blackledge
    B) Richie Lucas
    C) Tony Sacca
    D) Kerry Collins

4) Who was Penn State's quarterback in the 1987 Fiesta Bowl against Miami?

    A) Doug Strang
    B) Matt Knizner
    C) Tony Sacca
    D) John Shaffner

Overtime Bonus *4-Point Questions*

5) How many Big Ten teams did Penn State play prior to joining the conference?

    A) 5
    B) 6
    C) 8
    D) 10

6) What year were lights installed at Beaver Stadium?

    A) 1965
    B) 1978
    C) 1984
    D) 1987

7) How many times has PSU finished last in the Big Ten?

    A) 0
    B) 1
    C) 2
    D) 3

8) How many Penn State players had over 100 tackles in 2007?

    A) 1
    B) 2
    C) 3
    D) 4

9) What is the lowest final *AP* ranking for Penn State after holding the top ranking during the season?

A) 4th
B) 6th
C) 7th
D) 9th

10) What are the most points scored by Penn State in a single game?

A) 78
B) 89
C) 96
D) 109

Overtime Bonus Answer Key

1) D – Bob Higgins (19 years, 1930-48)

2) B – 4 (Penn State won every meeting from 1993-96.)

3) C – Tony Sacca (He was picked by the Cardinals in the second round of the 1992 NFL Draft.)

4) D – John Shaffner (He finished the night with 5 completions on 16 attempts for 53 yards and one interception.)

5) B – 6 (PSU played every member before 1993 except for Michigan, Minnesota, Indiana, and Northwestern.)

6) C – 1984 (The Nittany Lions are 6-6 all-time in night games at home.)

7) A – 0 (The worst finish for Penn State was 9th place in 2003 and 2004.)

8) B – 2 (Dan Connor led the team with 145 tackles and Sean Lee had 138 tackles.)

9) A – 4th (Penn State held the #1 spot for the last 4 weeks of the season before losing 7-14 to #2 Alabama in the 1979 Sugar Bowl.)

10) D – 109 (In 1920, PSU beat Lebanon Valley 109-7.)

Note: All answers valid as of the end of the 2007 season, unless otherwise indicated in the question itself.

Player / Team Score Sheet

Name:_____

First Quarter			Second Quarter			Third Quarter			Fourth Quarter			Overtime	
1		26	1		26	1		26	1		26	1	
2		27	2		27	2		27	2		27	2	
3		28	3		28	3		28	3		28	3	
4		29	4		29	4		29	4		29	4	
5		30	5		30	5		30	5		30	5	
6		31	6		31	6		31	6		31	6	
7		32	7		32	7		32	7		32	7	
8		33	8		33	8		33	8		33	8	
9		34	9		34	9		34	9		34	9	
10		35	10		35	10		35	10		35	10	
11		36	11		36	11		36	11		36		
12		37	12		37	12		37	12		37		
13		38	13		38	13		38	13		38		
14		39	14		39	14		39	14		39		
15		40	15		40	15		40	15		40		
16		41	16		41	16		41	16		41		
17		42	17		42	17		42	17		42		
18		43	18		43	18		43	18		43		
19		44	19		44	19		44	19		44		
20		45	20		45	20		45	20		45		
21		46	21		46	21		46	21		46		
22		47	22		47	22		47	22		47		
23		48	23		48	23		48	23		48		
24		49	24		49	24		49	24		49		
25		50	25		50	25		50	25		50		

___x 1 =____   ___x 2 =____   ___x 3 =____   ___x 4 =____   ___x 4 =____

Multiply total number correct by point value/quarter to calculate totals for each quarter.

Add total of all quarters below.

Total Points:_____

Thank you for playing Nittany Lionology Trivia Challenge.

Additional score sheets are available at:
www.TriviaGameBooks.com

85

Player / Team Score Sheet

Name:_____

First Quarter		Second Quarter		Third Quarter		Fourth Quarter		Overtime
1	26	1	26	1	26	1	26	1
2	27	2	27	2	27	2	27	2
3	28	3	28	3	28	3	28	3
4	29	4	29	4	29	4	29	4
5	30	5	30	5	30	5	30	5
6	31	6	31	6	31	6	31	6
7	32	7	32	7	32	7	32	7
8	33	8	33	8	33	8	33	8
9	34	9	34	9	34	9	34	9
10	35	10	35	10	35	10	35	10
11	36	11	36	11	36	11	36	
12	37	12	37	12	37	12	37	
13	38	13	38	13	38	13	38	
14	39	14	39	14	39	14	39	
15	40	15	40	15	40	15	40	
16	41	16	41	16	41	16	41	
17	42	17	42	17	42	17	42	
18	43	18	43	18	43	18	43	
19	44	19	44	19	44	19	44	
20	45	20	45	20	45	20	45	
21	46	21	46	21	46	21	46	
22	47	22	47	22	47	22	47	
23	48	23	48	23	48	23	48	
24	49	24	49	24	49	24	49	
25	50	25	50	25	50	25	50	
___x 1 =___		___x 2 =___		___x 3 =___		___x 4 =___		___x 4 =___

Multiply total number correct by point value/quarter to calculate totals for each quarter.

Add total of all quarters below.

Total Points:_____

Thank you for playing Nittany Lionology Trivia Challenge.

Additional score sheets are available at:
www.TriviaGameBooks.com